SMART WORDS
READER

Wheels
and Axles

Kathy Furgang

SCHOLASTIC INC.

What are SMART WORDS?

Smart Words are frequently used words that are critical to understanding concepts taught in the classroom. The more Smart Words a child knows, the more easily he or she will grasp important curriculum concepts. Smart Words Readers introduce these key words in a fun and motivational format while developing important literacy skills. Each new word is highlighted, defined in context, and reviewed. Engaging activities at the end of each chapter allow readers to practice the words they have learned.

ISBN 978-0-545-46706-3

Packaged by Q2A Bill Smith

Series Editor: Barbara M. Linde.

Copyright © 2013 by Scholastic Inc.

Picture Credit: t= top, b= bottom, l= left, r= right, c= center

Cover Page: Andrey N Bannov/Shutterstock.

Title Page: Bogdanhoda/Shutterstock.

Content Page: Maksim Shmeljov/Shutterstock.

4: Peter Albrektsen/Shutterstock; 5: Justasc/Shutterstock; 6: Sergei Bachlakov/Shutterstock; 7: George Dolgikh/Shutterstock; 8: Cbenjasuwan/Shutterstock; 9: Timothy Large/Shutterstock; 10: Photocami/Shutterstock; 11: Antonio Abrignani/Shutterstock; 12: Buida Nikita Yourievich/Shutterstock(c), Silverlining56/iStockphoto(b); 13: Thanomphong/Shutterstock; 14: Mr Jamsey/iStockphoto; 15: Natalya Kozyreva/iStockphoto; 16: Fotum/Shutterstock; 17: Vivid Pixels/Shutterstock; 18: Joe McNally/Getty Images News/Getty Images; 19: Christian Carroll/iStockphoto; 20: Sondra Paulson/iStockphoto; 21: Sipa Press/Rex Features; 22: MaszaS/Shutterstock; 24: Zbynek Jirousek/Shutterstock; 25: Scott Rothstein/iStockphoto; 28: Lynn Seeden/iStockphoto; 29: Losevsky Photo and Video/Shutterstock.

Q2A Bill Smith Art Bank: 23, 26, 27.

All rights reserved. Published by Scholastic Inc.

SCHOLASTIC and associated logos are trademarks and/or registered trademarks of Scholastic Inc.

12 11 10 9 8 7 6 5 4 3 2 1   13 14 15 16 17 18/0

Printed in the U.S.A.   40

First printing, January 2013

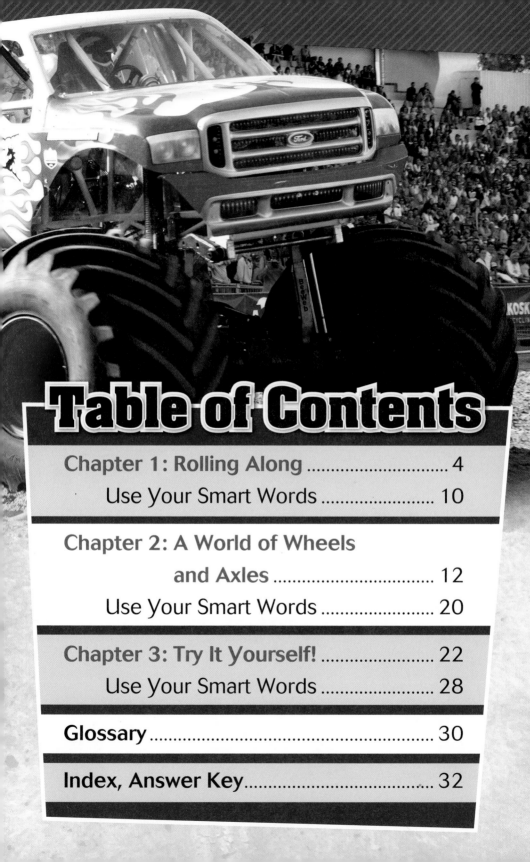

Table of Contents

Chapter 1

Rolling Along

Imagine you are at a monster-truck rally. A monster truck rolls along the track as people clap and cheer. The driver waves to the crowd. You notice the huge, shiny body of the truck. But the enormous **wheels and axles** that are under the body interest you the most. You want to learn all about them. Let's get started!

On a truck like this, a wheel is connected to each end of an axle.

axle

wheel

A wheel and axle is an example of a **simple machine**. A simple machine is a tool with few or no moving parts. It helps you push, pull, lift, lower, or cut an object.

A wheel is a stiff disc. It is connected at the center to a stiff rod called an axle. The wheel **rotates**, or turns, around the axle.

Move It

In science, the word **force** refers to a push or a pull. The weight of the object you want to move is called the **load**. Imagine a vehicle, like this race car, without wheels. It would look like a big box sitting on the ground. Now imagine trying to push this car along the road.

The car would rub against the ground and create **friction**. This friction would make the car hard to move. What happens when you put wheels under the car? The wheels roll as the car moves, so there is not as much friction between the car and the road. The wheels make moving the car easier.

Race cars reach speeds of more than 100 miles (161 kilometers) per hour and make sharp turns on a track — thanks to wheels and axles!

Steer It

Think about trying to move a 2-ton car left or right. Whew — it's hard! A special wheel called a steering wheel makes the job easier. This wheel and axle change the **direction** of the car's force.

wheel

axle

The steering wheel is connected to an axle called the steering column. This connects to parts inside the car that turn the wheels. In order to turn left smoothly, the left wheels must turn more than the right wheels.

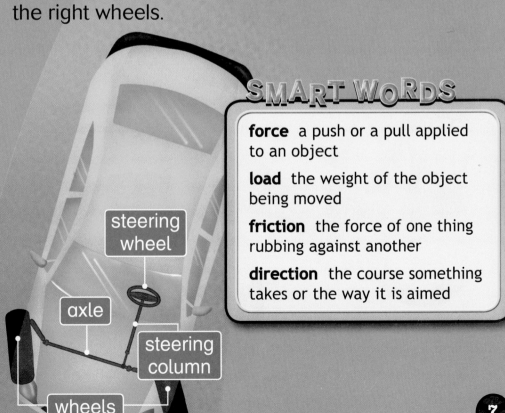

steering wheel

axle

steering column

wheels

SMART WORDS

force a push or a pull applied to an object

load the weight of the object being moved

friction the force of one thing rubbing against another

direction the course something takes or the way it is aimed

Bike with It

Have you noticed that you can move faster on a bike than you can by walking or running? That's because bikes use wheels and axles to make moving your body easier.

Each wheel of a bike turns on an axle. The pedals rotate around an axle, too. As you push the pedals, the force is sent to the rear wheel by the chain. The bike moves forward.

rear wheel

People use bikes for fun and transportation.

front wheel

chain

axle

pedal

Speed with It

We say something is in **motion** when it is moving. **Speed** is how fast or slow the object moves.

The speed that a bicycle moves depends on the force applied to the pedals. Push down on the pedals quickly and the bike will move at a faster speed. Push down on the pedals slowly and the bike will move at a slower speed.

SMART WORDS

motion the action or process of moving

speed how fast or slow something moves

The average riding speed of a bike is between 10-15 miles (16-24 kilometers) per hour. But a racing bike can reach speeds of over 30 miles (48 kilometers) per hour!

Use your SMART WORDS

Answer each question with a Smart Word.

wheel and axle	simple machine
rotates force	load friction
direction	motion speed

1. What is the weight of an object being moved called?
2. What is another word for a push or a pull?
3. What term is used for a tool with few or no moving parts?
4. Which part of a bike or car helps it to move?
5. What term describes how fast something moves?
6. What is it called when something moves around a center point?
7. What is the name for the course something takes or the way it is aimed?
8. What is the result of two objects rubbing against each other?
9. What word describes the action or process of moving?

Answers on page 32

Talk Like a Scientist

You have a stack of newspapers that you want to move to the front curb for recycling. Use your Smart Words to explain how using a wagon will make the stack of papers easier to move.

Did You Know?

No one knows for sure who invented the wheelbarrow. Some think the Chinese invented it, while others think the Greeks did.

That's Amazing!

General Chuko Liang of China invented one type of wheelbarrow over 2,000 years ago. He used the wheelbarrow to move supplies and wounded soldiers.

Good to Know

Starting around 1200 A.D., people in Europe used the wheelbarrow to carry goods for mining, building, and farming.

Chapter 2

A World of Wheels and Axles

Did you know that a doorknob is a wheel and axle? The knob is the wheel. When you turn the knob, the axle applies force to the load, which is a latch inside the door. The force lifts the latch. Then you can pull or push the door open.

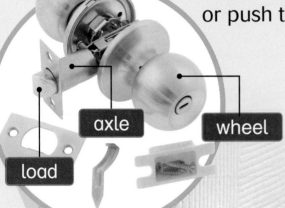

load

axle

wheel

The wheel of a doorknob moves a little bit and does not make a complete turn to work.

Cranks are also wheels and axles. Pencil sharpeners, windows, and ice-cream machines all use cranks.

The load is on the axle. The crank acts as the wheel and turns the axle. There's a handle at the other end of the crank. When you apply a force to the handle, the crank rotates. The force you apply is called **effort**. The longer the crank is, the less effort you need to turn it. The crank gives **mechanical advantage** because it reduces the effort needed to move the load.

SMART WORDS

effort the pushing, pulling, or turning force that is made to move something

mechanical advantage when a simple machine lets you use less effort to do work

Big Wheels

Look at the wheels on the stroller. If you draw a line through the center of the wheel from one side to the other, you have marked the **diameter**. The diameter is a measurement of the wheel's size. The larger the wheel's diameter, the longer it takes for the wheel to make one complete turn around its axle.

The back of the stroller has two wheels attached to one axle. In the front, one wheel is attached to one axle.

diameter

diameter

Little Wheels

Now compare the large stroller to this small one. The wheels on the toy stroller are much smaller. They have a smaller diameter. Suppose the strollers are both pushed at the same speed. It takes a much shorter time for the small wheels to make one complete turn around an axle than the large wheels. If both strollers were pushed the same **distance**, or space between two places, the smaller wheels would have turned many more times than the large ones.

SMART WORDS

diameter measurement across a circle through its center point

distance the space between two places

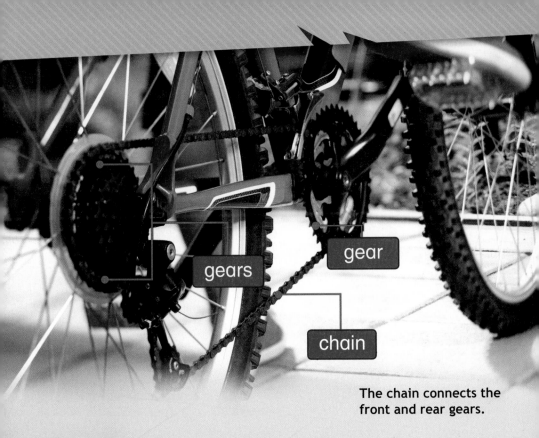

gears

gear

chain

The chain connects the front and rear gears.

Gears

A **gear** is a wheel with teeth along the outside edge. The gear is also attached to the axle. The teeth of the gear grab on to a chain, the teeth of another gear, or another object to help move a load.

Mountain bikes use many gears of different sizes. Some gears help the rider move faster on a flat surface. Other gears allow the rider to climb hills with less effort.

Sometimes gears are connected to each other and one makes another turn. When one gear moves, the gear it connects to moves in the opposite direction. The gear that is turned is called the **driver**. The one that turns as a result is called the **follower**.

A clock uses many gears. Each hand of the clock that the gears move is a load. Without a clock's gears, the second hand, minute hand, and hour hand would not be able to move at the correct speed.

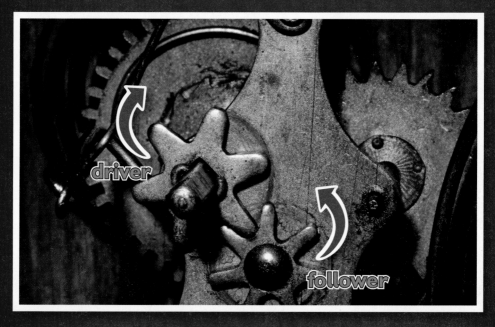

These gears are for a large clock.

SMART WORDS

gear a wheel with teeth along the outside edge
driver the gear that is turned to move another gear next to it
follower the gear next to a driver that turns

Wheels and Axles on the Job

Have you ever been to an amusement park and wondered who creates the rides? Thank an engineer! Roller coaster engineers use math and science to design roller coasters that are safe and fun. They must understand how forces and motion work.

The engineers know how **gravity** pulls on the load, or the cars, as they go downhill. They use this knowledge to plan the height of the hills and loops, and the distance between them, so the cars go faster or slower. They plan carefully so riders will get a thrill but still stay in their seats!

Next time you are having fun on a roller coaster, think about the serious science that makes it work.

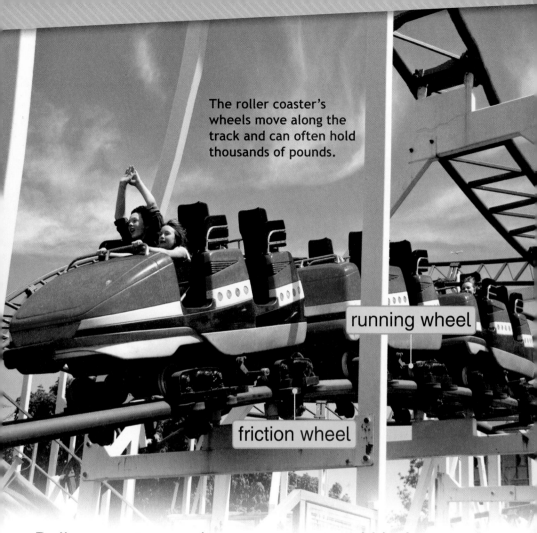

The roller coaster's wheels move along the track and can often hold thousands of pounds.

running wheel

friction wheel

Roller coaster engineers use several kinds of wheels and axles when they design roller coasters. The running wheels are on top of the track and guide the cars. Friction wheels on the side keep the cars on the track during sharp turns. Roller coasters with upside-down loops have upstop wheels to keep the cars in place.

SMART WORD

gravity a pulling force between objects

Use your SMART WORDS

Match each description to the correct Smart Word.

effort   mechanical advantage   diameter

distance   gear   driver   follower   gravity

1. when a simple machine lets you use less effort to do work
2. a wheel with teeth along the outside edge
3. length from one side of a circle to the other, passing through the center
4. the gear that turns to move another gear next to it
5. the pushing, pulling, or turning force that is made to move something
6. the space between two places
7. a pulling force between objects
8. the attached gear that turns

Answers on page 32

Talk Like a Scientist

You are an engineer who is designing a new amusement-park ride. Draw the ride and describe how a wheel and axle can be used in your design. Use Smart Words to explain the different forces at work in your ride.

SMART FACTS

Did You Know?

The world's fastest roller coaster is the Formula Rossa on Yas Island, part of the United Arab Emirates.

Zipping Along!

The roller coaster reaches its top speed in less than five seconds and makes a sharp 70-degree turn. Riders wear goggles to go on the ride!

That's Amazing!

Formula Rossa's top speed is 149 miles (240 kilometers) per hour. That's as fast as the real Ferrari Formula One race car that the roller coaster is designed to look like.

Chapter 3

Try It Yourself!

Now you know that a wheel and axle is a simple machine that makes it easier to move things over a distance. It's time to have some fun and try out your new knowledge. Think like an engineer and use wheels and axles to solve problems.

Making pinwheels is a good way to learn about how a wheel and axle works. What do you think will happen if you spin a pinwheel made equally of two different colors? You can make a **hypothesis** to explain what you think will happen. A hypothesis is an idea that has to be tested to prove it is right. Try it to find out if your hypothesis is correct. To form your hypothesis, think about what you know about wheels and axles.

SMART WORD

hypothesis an idea that has to be tested to prove it is right

Make Pinwheels

Get Started

1. Trace the top of each can on the poster board. Cut out the three circles.

2. Use the ruler to mark the center of each circle and draw four evenly spaced straight lines across the diameter and through the center.

3. Color the spaces, alternating between yellow and blue. Press hard to make the colors dark.

4. Straighten a small paper clip and poke it through the center of the largest circle. Poke the paper clip all the way through the pencil eraser as shown.

5. Spin the wheel quickly. Observe the speed and color of the wheel.

6. Repeat Steps 4 and 5 for the other two wheels. Which wheel turns most before slowing down? How does the speed of the pinwheel affect the color you see?

Answers on page 32

Use materials you have at home or school. Ask an adult for help. Wear goggles or other safety equipment. Take photographs, draw pictures, or keep notes as you work.

Make Gears

A model is a smaller version of a full-size object. When you make a model of something we learned about in science class, you get a better idea of how something works. You can make a model of gears by using simple objects like poster-board circles and toothpicks. Toothpicks act like the teeth of the gears. You can add the axle by putting a paper brad, also called a fastener, through each circle and then turning the wheel with your fingers.

SMART WORD

model a small object made to look like a full-size object

Models work like real things but are smaller. They can be made of simple objects.

Get Started

What You Need

- two small pieces of poster board (the same or different colors)
- scissors
- 20 toothpicks
- glue
- empty cardboard box, such as a tissue box
- pencil
- two paper brads (also called paper fasteners)

1. Cut out two circles from the poster board: one with a 2-inch diameter and one with a 4-inch diameter.

2. Glue eight toothpicks on the 2-inch circle. Space them evenly and make sure the toothpicks stick out from the circle.

3. Glue twelve toothpicks on the 4-inch circle. Space them evenly and make sure the toothpicks stick out from the circle.

4. Put a paper brad through the center of one circle and through the top of the box. Spread out the prongs to keep the brad in place.

5. Put a paper brad through the center of the other circle and through the side of the box. Spread out the prongs to keep the brad in place. Make sure the toothpicks on each circle touch each other.

6. Turn one gear clockwise. What happens to the other gear?

paper brads

4-inch circle

toothpick

paper brad

2-inch circle

Answers on page 32

Make a Race Car

One of the most fun uses for wheels and axles is making toys that roll. When you **investigate** in science, you examine something in detail. Let's investigate what kinds of wheels and axles will make a toy car roll best.

Get Started

1. The cardboard will be the body of your car. Cut the piece of cardboard to a width of 5 to 7 inches (13 to 18 centimeters). The width of the cardboard should be slightly smaller than the length of your wooden pencils. Choose the length you want for your car body.

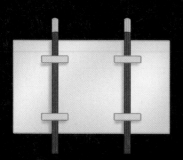

2. The wooden pencils will serve as axles. Tape or glue the wooden pencils across the width of the underside of the cardboard. Put one pencil near the front of the body and the other pencil near the rear of the body, just like the axles on a real car.

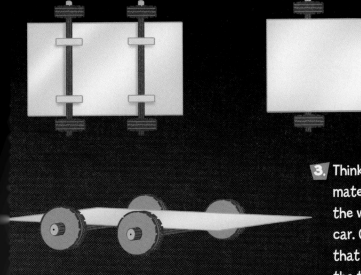

3. Think about th
materials to us
the wheels of y
car. Consider h
that material
the toy car mo

4. Make a chart listing the good points
and the problems of each material.

5. Choose one or more materials and make the wheels. An adult may r
to help you create the right size hole for your wheels to attach th
to the axle.

6. Test your car. Write your observations about the wheels on your c

Materials	Good Points	Problems	Observations
Rubber wheels	Fast	May not be strong	Bumpy ride
Wooden wheels	Strong	May not be fast	Not fast
Cardboard wheels	May be slow	May bend	Not strong
Plastic wheels	Fast	May not be strong	Fast

SMART WORD

investigate to examine something in detail

Answers on page 3

Use your SMART WORDS

Read each clue. Choose the Smart Word it describes.

> hypothesis   model   investigate

1. This means to examine something in detail.

2. This is an idea that has to be tested to prove it is right.

3. This is a small object made to look like a full-size object.

Answers on page 32

Talk Like a Scientist

Think about the car you built. Did it move and work like you expected? What would you do differently if you could build the car again? Use Smart Words to describe your plan.

SMART FACTS

A Welcome Invention

Thinking like an engineer helped Bernard Sadow invent the first wheeled suitcase in 1970. Instead of dragging a heavy bag, he could wheel it in comfort.

Did You Know?

Once people tried using the wheeled luggage, they liked it. Before long, airports were full of wheeled bags.

It Worked Out Well

Today, everything is on wheels, including duffle bags and kids' backpacks! The wheels used to come in plain black, but now you can get them in a rainbow of colors.

Glossary

diameter measurement across a circle through its center point

direction the course something takes or the way it is aimed

distance the space between two places

driver the gear that is turned to move another gear next to it

effort the pushing, pulling, or turning force that is made to move something

follower the gear next to a driver that turns

force a push or a pull applied to an object

friction the force of one thing rubbing against another

gear a wheel with teeth along the outside edge

gravity a pulling force between objects

hypothesis an idea that has to be tested to prove it is right

investigate to examine something in detail

load the weight of the object being moved

mechanical advantage when a simple machine lets you use less effort to do work

model a small object made to look like a full-size object

motion the action or process of moving

rotates moves around a center point

simple machine a tool with few or no moving parts

speed how fast or slow something moves

wheel and axle a simple machine made up of a stiff disc called a wheel connected to a stiff rod called an axle

Index

SMART WORDS Answer Key

Page 10
1. load, 2. force, 3. simple machine, 4. wheel and axle, 5. speed, 6. rotates, 7. direction, 8. friction, 9. motion

Page 20
1. mechanical advantage, 2. gear, 3. diameter, 4. driver, 5. effort, 6. distance, 7. gravity, 8. follower

Page 23
The smallest wheel makes the most complete turns. As the wheels spin, your eye will see the yellow and blue as green, especially for the smallest wheel.

Page 25
If one gear is moved clockwise, the second gear will move counterclockwise.

Page 26–27
The material used on the wheels will affect the speed and durability of the car. Rubber wheels may move faster than wooden or metal wheels, though wood may be stronger. Axles must be made of materials thick enough to make the wheels stable.

Page 28
1. investigate, 2. hypothesis, 3. model